BROKEN FIXTURES IN A REFLECTING MIRROR

By

Carmila T.

Unspoken Pages Publishing

Copyright © 2026 by Carmila T.

All rights reserved.

No part of this book may be reproduced, distributed, or transmitted in any form or by any means, including photocopying, recording, or other electronic or mechanical methods, without the prior written permission of the author, except in the case of brief quotations used in reviews or for educational purposes.

This book is a work of nonfiction based on the author's personal experiences. Names, details, and identifying characteristics may have been changed to protect the privacy of individuals.

Scripture quotations are taken from the Holy Bible. Unless otherwise noted, all scripture references are from the King James Version (KJV).

Published by
Unspoken Pages Publishing

First Edition

Printed in the United States of America

TABLE OF CONTENTS

INTRODUCTION

Welcome to the Journey

This book is for the women who have survived what felt impossible. For the women whose childhoods were filled with chaos, silence, neglect, abuse, and unanswered questions. For the women who feel like the world never truly saw them like their pain, their tears, and their struggle went unnoticed.

I want you to know something before you read another word: you are seen. You are heard. You are not alone.

My story is my truth. The broken fixtures in my reflecting mirror and I share it not to relive the pain, but to show you that healing is possible, even when the world fails you. From my earliest memories of a chaotic home, to being taken by DCF, to surviving neglect, abuse, and betrayal, this book traces the path of my life from childhood through young adulthood.

You may recognize your own pain in my story. You may see reflections of your struggles, your silence, or the lies you were told about your worth. And I want you to know: the lies are not true. Your value is not determined by the adults who failed you, the circumstances you endured, or the world that tried to tell you otherwise.

This book is faith-centered because my faith has been the one constant thread through every fracture in my life. It is the light that guided me when I felt lost, the strength that carried me when I wanted to give up, and the hope that reminded me I was never forgotten.

2 Corinthians 4:7 says:

“But we have this treasure in jars of clay, to show that the surpassing power belongs to God and not to us.”

Even in our brokenness, even when we feel fragile and small, God’s treasure resides within us. This is my story, but it is also a guide for women like you women who have faced trauma, who have survived, and who are ready to reclaim their worth, their voice, and their life.

As you read, I hope you will feel safe, seen, and understood. I hope you will find encouragement in these pages, reminders that you are more than the pain you endured, and the courage to take steps toward healing.

Welcome. You are in the right place. Your story matters. Your life matters. And God sees you.

Chapter 1

The First Crack

A Childhood in Shadows

I remember lying awake at night, listening to the quiet hum of the world outside my window. The stars shone softly, and the air smelled like rain. In those rare moments, I allowed myself to imagine a life where things felt safe, a life where I didn't have to constantly brace for chaos.

But the reality of my home was different. It was loud, unpredictable, and emotionally silent. My mom struggled with addiction, and my dad was barely there, sometimes physically present, but never fully present in my life.

There were days when we didn't have enough to eat. Days when it felt like we were the adults in the house, forced to care for ourselves and each other in ways no child should ever have to. Eventually, someone reported our living conditions, and DCF came. I was taken from my mom. A woman I still loved, even in the middle of chaos I didn't understand.

Being removed from the only home I had ever known felt like stepping into another kind of uncertainty, one that promised protection but came with its own fears.

Living With My Grandparents

I was placed in the care of my grandparents on my father's side. They did what they could to give me stability, love, and safety. It wasn't perfect, but it was the first place I truly felt protected, even if only a little.

For the first time in my young life, I had people around me who were consistent. I had meals I could rely on, a bed that was mine, and some sense of what it meant to feel safe.

Even there, cracks had already begun to form. I had learned early that my voice could be dangerous, that emotions could bring more harm than help, and that survival often meant quiet endurance.

The Visit That Broke Me

While living with my grandparents, I was allowed to visit my maternal grandmother. I trusted that it would be a safe place a moment to see family, maybe even a brief respite from the world that often felt harsh and unforgiving.

But during that visit, my mom came to pick me up. What was supposed to be a brief reunion turned into something that would leave lasting scars. I was molested. I was scared, confused, and alone.

A place that should have felt safe… a home, family, became another fracture in my spirit.

That experience taught me early lessons about survival:

- I could not rely fully on adults.
- My feelings were secondary.
- Speaking up could bring danger.
- Silence could sometimes keep me alive.

The Schoolyard Shadows

Even outside the home, the world didn't feel safe. At school, I faced another kind of pain: exclusion and ridicule.

I was teased for not having what other children had the clothes, shoes, and hairstyles. I was reminded every day of what I couldn't afford.

And the teasing didn't stop there. I was picked on for the color of my skin, for how dark I was, for something I had no control over. The words cut deeper than any slap, deeper than any silence at home. They whispered the same lie I already felt inside:

"You are not enough. You don't belong. You are different, and that is wrong."

At school, I carried the weight of two worlds: a fractured home and a world that judged me for what I could not change. I felt invisible, alone, and unseen.

The Lies I Began to Believe

In a home filled with chaos, neglect, and abuse, and a schoolyard full of ridicule, I began to believe lies about myself:

"I am nothing. I am worthless. No one will ever care. I am a burden. I am not enough."

Even as a child, I internalized these lies. They whispered to me in quiet moments, in the silences that felt louder than any shouting, in the spaces where no one chose me, where no one noticed me.

And yet, even then, God was with me. Even in the cracks, even when the adults and peers around me failed, He saw me.

2 Corinthians 4:7 reminds us that fragile jars of clay can still hold treasure. That treasure was me. My spirit. My heart. My resilience.

The Cracks Become a Pattern

As I grew, I began to take on roles to survive:

- The strong one
- The responsible one
- The fixer
- The peacemaker

I didn't know how to need anyone. Needing felt dangerous. So, I became dependable instead. I became the one who carried the weight so no one else would notice the cracks.

People praised me for it, but they didn't see the little girl inside. The one who never learned how to feel safe without performing, the one who was quietly fractured, the one who sacrificed herself to keep her siblings together.

To the Woman Reading This

If you grew up:

- In a home that was chaotic, unpredictable, and emotionally empty
- With adults who were struggling or absent
- Experiencing abuse or neglect that left invisible scars
- Feeling unseen, unheard, or unchosen
- Being judged, teased, or excluded for things beyond your control

I need you to hear this clearly:

You were adapting.

You were not weak.

You were not alone, even when it felt that way.

You were surviving.

And God never mistook your survival for all you were meant to be. He saw the little girl. He still does.

Even in the cracks, even in the brokenness, He carried treasure through you.

PAUSE & REFLECT

What are your ready to release so you can heal?

Write your thoughts below:

Reminder: *Your breaking point was not your ending.*

Chapter 2

Survival Mode

When Safe Was Taken from Me

The Choice That Carried a Cost

After years of stability with my grandparents, my life shifted again. My aunt decided she would take over raising me and my siblings.

My siblings were leaving, and I could not bear the thought of being separated from them.

I made a choice. I went with her.

Not because it felt safe. Not because it felt loving. Not because it was right.

I went because I loved my siblings more than I loved my own safety.

Even as a child, I understood sacrifice. I understood that love sometimes meant putting yourself last.

But this choice carried a cost I did not understand at the time.

I resent it now. I resent the harm I endured simply for trying to keep my family together. I resent the nights I cried alone, the times I had nowhere safe to turn, and the moments I wondered if anyone would ever care.

And yet, even in that resentment, there was truth: I acted out of love, even when the world could not see it. God saw it. He knew the heart behind my choice, even when my life was broken around me.

The Home That Should Have Protected Me

At my aunt's house, the rules of survival I had learned with my grandparents had to start over.

The adults in this home didn't know how to love a child. They didn't know how to nurture, guide, or protect.

Instead, I was treated like a stumbling block, a punching bag for anger and control. I was told I was worthless, that I would never amount to anything, that I was nothing.

Even the small things became battles: hygiene, school clothes, daily necessities. I was expected to figure everything out on my own.

Every morning, I woke up wondering:

- Will today be better?
- Will someone notice I need help?
- Will someone choose me for once?

And the answer was almost always no.

Being treated like trash in a home that should have nurtured me left a mark. It was confusing and heartbreaking, I knew what family *should* feel like, but I was learning over and over that it was not my reality.

The Streets and Isolation

Sometimes, when life at my aunt's home became unbearable, I was cast out, figuratively and literally.

I remember being thrown into the streets like a ragdoll, ignored, dirty water thrown on me, left to fend for myself while still in high school. The streets smelled of fear and desperation. Every step I took felt heavy, like the world itself was pressing me down.

No one came looking for me. Not my father. Not my mother. Not the system. I learned early that if I wanted to survive, I had to depend on myself, because no one else would.

Isolation became my constant companion. I walked to school alone. I ate alone. I cried alone. I carried my pain quietly, like a secret treasure that no one could hold but me.

Loving a Mother Who Couldn't Love Me Back

Eventually, I returned to my mother.

I watched her do the same things she had when I was a child: drugs, unstable relationships, neglect. She spoke to me as though I were nothing, yet I still loved her. I still longed for the mother I never had, the woman who could have kept me safe.

This love was confusing. It hurt. But it also taught me something: love is bigger than circumstances. God planted the seed of love in me even when the world told me I was unlovable.

When I Tried to Leave

I tried to escape the only way I could imagine, I attempted to end my life multiple times.

The pain was so heavy that death seemed easier than life.

And yet… I woke up.

Even in my deepest despair, God was there. Even when I felt invisible, abandoned, and worthless, He preserved me.

I began to see that even in survival mode, even when the world had given up on me, God had not.

I clung to verses like 2 Corinthians 4:8–9:

“We are hard pressed on every side but not crushed; perplexed, but not in despair; persecuted but not abandoned; struck down but not destroyed.”

That verse became more than words on a page. It became my reality.

I was hard pressed… by neglect, by abuse, by abandonment.

I was perplexed…. confused about why the people who were supposed to love me did not.

I was persecuted…. emotionally and mentally attacked in places that should have felt safe.

I was struck down…. knocked flat by betrayal and despair.

But I was not destroyed.

Somehow, I kept waking up.

Somehow, my heart kept beating.

Somehow, I kept going to school, kept surviving, kept breathing.

Looking back now, I understand something I didn't understand then: survival is not weakness. Survival is strength under pressure.

Living in Survival Mode

Survival mode meant I was always alert.

It meant I listened carefully to tones of voice.

It meant I studied facial expressions.

It meant I learned how to shrink myself to avoid attention.

It meant I became emotionally guarded because vulnerability felt dangerous.

I stopped expecting kindness.

I stopped believing someone would rescue me.

I stopped thinking I deserved protection.

Instead, I became my own protector.

I learned how to read a room in seconds.

I learned when to speak and when to stay silent.

I learned how to swallow tears so no one would use them against me.

But survival mode also came with a cost.

When you live in survival mode too long, you forget how to rest.

You forget how to trust.

You forget what peace feels like.

Your body may be alive, but your heart feels constantly braced for impact.

The Burden of Feeling Unwanted

One of the heaviest parts of that season wasn't just the mistreatment, it was the feeling that I was a burden.

When my father saw my living situation and I asked for help, and he told me he needed to talk to his girlfriend and would "let me know," something inside me shifted.

I felt small.

Disposable.

Secondary.

As if my safety depended on whether someone else approved.

That moment told me a lie I carried for years:

"You are too much."

"You are inconvenient."

"You are not worth choosing."

Those lies dug deep.

But now I know the truth: I was never too much. I was a child asking for help.

The Resentment I Had to Face

As I grew older, I had to confront something uncomfortable, resentment.

I resented my aunt.

I resented the adults who failed me.

I resented my parents.

I even resented myself for making the choice to go.

I asked myself:

Why did I sacrifice my safety?

Why did I think I had to save everyone?

Why did I believe my needs didn't matter?

But healing forced me to see something gently and honestly:

I was a child making the best decision I could with the love I had.

That love, the love for my siblings, was not weakness. It was strength. It was loyalty. It was sacrifice.

And even though the world mishandled that sacrifice, God did not.

He saw the heart behind my decision.

He saw the tears no one wiped away.

He saw the nights I wished I would not wake up.

And He kept me anyway.

Still Here

Survival mode was brutal.

It hardened parts of me.

It wounded parts of me.

It left scars I am still learning to understand.

But it also built resilience in me that cannot be shaken.

It taught me how to endure.

It taught me how to adapt.

It taught me that even when everything around me collapses, I can stand.

Most importantly, it proved something undeniable:

I am still here.

The girl who was neglected.

The girl who was thrown aside.

The girl who tried to leave this world.

She survived.

And survival was not the end of my story.

It was only the beginning.

PAUSE & REFLECT:

Are you still surviving…. Or are you ready to start healing?

Write your thoughts below:

Reminder: *You don't have to stay in survival mode.*

Chapter 3
Fighting to Be Seen

Hiding in Plain Sight,

High school was a paradox: I was surrounded by people, yet I felt completely alone. To the outside world, I laughed, joked, played basketball, and acted like a carefree teen. But inside, I was carrying burdens too heavy for any child, let alone a teenager. My home was chaos, my mom was caught in drugs and destructive patterns, and my siblings and I had been separated, not by choice, but by force.

Being at school felt like a temporary sanctuary, a place where I could pretend to be normal, where no one knew the storm, I carried. I smiled constantly, not because I was happy, but because hiding my pain was the only way I felt safe. I laughed and played around to get attention, to feel seen, to feel like I mattered.

But beneath the smiles, fear and anxiety lurked. I didn't dare speak about what was happening at home because I didn't know what consequences awaited me when I returned. I had learned early that silence could be survival.

Seeking Validation

I sought validation wherever I could find it, from classmates, teachers, friends, even romantic interests. I craved reassurance that I mattered, that I was enough, and that someone could see me beyond the bruises, the scars, and the chaos of my life.

For a while, I thought I found it. I met someone in high school who said the things I wanted to hear, who made me feel wanted and cared for. But what I didn't realize at the time was that he wanted only to use me, manipulate me, and control me. The betrayal cut deep. It made me angry, mistrustful, and more determined to protect myself. I hated that I had allowed myself to be vulnerable, but I also hated the reality of living in a world where people couldn't be trusted.

Anger as Armor

I carried anger like armor. I was defensive and quick to react when I felt slighted or misunderstood. Even when people weren't actually targeting me, I felt attacked, because I had learned early that the world could be cruel, that words could wound, and that no one would protect me.

I refused to let myself be treated like trash, but often, the majority ruled. I learned that fighting everyone at once was impossible, so I learned to pick my battles and protect what little of myself I could.

Fractured Family, Fractured Heart

By this point, my siblings and I had drifted apart. We had gone separate ways, not because we wanted to, but because circumstances forced us apart. The bond that had once felt unbreakable had been tested by neglect, separation, and survival.

It was painful to watch us grow distant. My love for them remained, but the circumstances made it impossible to feel whole as a family. Loneliness became my shadow, always present, even in moments of fleeting happiness.

Finding Glimpses of Hope

Amid all this pain, there were small moments of clarity. Slowly, I began to realize that some people liked me for who I truly was, not the performance I put on to hide my pain. That realization was revolutionary: I didn't always have to try so hard to be loved or seen.

Basketball, laughter, and play became more than just attention-seeking, they were reminders that I could find joy even in the midst of hardship, even in a world that had shown me little mercy.

Faith in the Shadows

Even when I felt abandoned, even when trust had been shattered, I knew God had not abandoned me. My faith became my secret strength, the one constant that reminded me I was never truly alone.

Psalm 34:18 says:

"The Lord is close to the brokenhearted and saves those who are crushed in spirit."

I clung to that verse fiercely. In the hallways of my school, on the basketball court, in laughter and in tears, God was my witness. He knew my pain, and He reminded me that my worth was never defined by the chaos around me.

Reflections for the Reader

To the women reading this: if you have ever felt unseen, unheard, or undervalued, if you have ever hidden your pain behind a smile, know this:

- You are worthy of being seen and loved just as you are.
- Your pain does not define your value.
- Trust in God's presence; He sees what the world cannot.

Sometimes survival means hiding, laughing, or playing a role. But in those moments, your resilience is building the foundation for the woman you are meant to become. Even when the world doesn't notice, God sees. Even when others fail you, He does not.

PAUSE & REFLECT:

Where in your life have you felt unseen or unheard?

Write your thoughts below:

Reminder: *You deserve to be seen, fully and authentically.*

Chapter 4

Broken Mirrors, Hidden Scars

Born Into Fragmentation

I was the fifth child out of nine.

But we were never nine together.

We were nine in blood, but not in household. Not in memory. Not in shared birthdays or Christmas mornings. Only three of us ever lived under the same roof at one time. The others were taken at birth, and were older than us and went their wan way, scattered into different homes, different lives, different stories.

We were siblings divided before we ever had the chance to become a family.

That reality left a quiet ache inside of me. I often wondered what it would have been like to grow up together, to share secrets, to fight and make up, to protect one another. Instead, we were separated pieces of the same broken mirror.

And somewhere in the middle of that fragmentation, I became the black sheep.

Not because I was rebellious.

Not because I was evil.

Not because I lacked value.

But because I was the one who felt everything.

I was the one who questioned.

The one who longed.

The one who noticed what others tried to ignore.

And in families shaped by trauma, the child who sees too much often becomes the problem.

Watching My Father Choose Everyone Else

There is a specific kind of wound that comes from watching a parent give their attention to everyone but you.

I saw my father with different women. I saw him invest time, laughter, energy, things I desperately needed. I watched him build connections, but not with me.

I wasn't asking for perfection.

I wasn't asking for wealth.

I wasn't even asking for grand gestures.

I was asking to be chosen.

And he didn't.

A father's absence creates questions a child does not know how to answer:

- What is wrong with me?
- Why am I not enough?
- Why does everyone else get the version of him I never receive?

Even when he was physically present, emotionally he was unreachable. And that distance taught me something dangerous: that love must be earned… and even then, it might not come.

But God began whispering something different to my spirit long before I understood it:

You were chosen before your father ever had the chance to reject you.

The Violation of Innocence

There are some wounds that do not leave bruises but leave deep imprints on the soul.

In my aunt's home, discipline was not correction, it was humiliation. It was control.

There were moments when I was supposed to be getting chastised for getting into trouble at school, but instead, something far darker lingered in the air. Her husband would look at me in ways that no grown man should ever look at a child. There were moments when I felt exposed in more ways than one, unsafe, confused, aware that something was wrong but too young to fully understand it.

No child should ever feel their innocence being threatened inside a home that is supposed to protect them.

The shame was heavy.

The confusion was suffocating.

The silence was deafening.

I did not have language for what was happening.

I only knew I felt small.

I only knew I wanted to disappear.

When adults violate boundaries, physically, emotionally, or spiritually, it plants seeds of distortion. It makes a child question their worth. It twists their understanding of safety.

But what the enemy meant to distort, God kept covered.

Even when I felt exposed, Heaven saw me clothed in dignity.

Even when I felt powerless, Heaven recorded every injustice.

Even when I felt alone, Heaven stood guard.

Psalm 34:18 says, *"The Lord is close to the brokenhearted and saves those who are crushed in spirit."*

I did not know it then, but God was close.

The Weight of Being the "Different" One

Being the fifth of nine but not truly belonging anywhere shaped how I saw myself.

I was too much in some spaces.

Too quiet in others.

Too emotional.

Too sensitive.

Too different.

The black sheep label followed me like a shadow.

In families built on instability, the child who doesn't adapt to dysfunction becomes the outsider. I could not normalize chaos. I could not pretend neglect didn't hurt. I could not silence the ache for something better.

So, I became "the problem."

But what they called rebellion was discernment.

What they called attitude was pain.

What they called weakness was actually awareness.

And what they rejected, God was refining.

Joseph was the favored son and became hated.

David was overlooked in the field.

Esther was an orphan in exile.

God has always had a pattern of choosing the unlikely one.

The black sheep often becomes the breakthrough.

Fragmented Family, Unbroken Calling

Although my siblings and I were scattered, there was still something sacred about our shared bloodline. Even if we did not grow up together, we were connected by survival.

Three of us shared space.

The rest were taken at birth.

All of us were shaped by the same storm.

And yet, I began to realize something powerful:

Fragmented beginnings do not determine finished outcomes.

God does not require perfect families to create purposeful lives.

I was not forgotten in the shuffle.

I was not misplaced in the order.

I was not an accident in the lineup of nine.

I was number five by birth.

But I was chosen first in Heaven.

From Black Sheep to Set Apart

For years, I resented being different.

Now I see it was protection.

If I had blended in, I might have accepted what was destroying us.

If I had felt fully comfortable in dysfunction, I might have stayed there.

If I had not felt the sting of rejection, I might never have searched for God's acceptance.

Being the black sheep kept my spirit from settling.

It made me hungry for truth.

Hungry for safety.

Hungry for a Father who does not divide His attention.

And when I finally encountered God, not just as a concept but as a covering, I understood something that changed everything:

I was never unwanted.

I was never unseen.

I was never unchosen.

Men may have overlooked me.

Adults may have mishandled me.

Family may have misunderstood me.

But Heaven never misidentified me.

Closing Reflection

Chapter 2 was survival.

Chapter 3 was awakening to God's preservation.

Chapter 4 is revelation.

The revelation that:

- My position in the birth order was not random.
- My siblings' fragmentation did not erase my identity.

- ❖ The inappropriate glances and unsafe moments did not define my worth.
- ❖ My father's choices did not determine my value.

I was not the black sheep.

I was the marked one.

Marked for survival.

Marked for healing.

Marked for purpose.

Marked by God.

And what was meant to silence me…

will become the testimony that sets others free.

What I thought were signs of damage were actually evidence of survival.

Broken mirrors may distort reflection,

but they cannot erase identity.

Hidden scars may ache,

but they also testify that you healed enough to keep living.

Chapter 2 was survival mode.

Chapter 3 was recognizing preservation.

Chapter 4 is understanding the internal damage, and the quiet grace that kept me from completely shattering.

I was cracked.

I was cut.

I was confused.

But I was never abandoned by God.

And even in a house full of broken mirrors,

He never lost sight of who I truly was.

PAUSE & REFLECT:

What parts of yourself have you been hiding?

Write your thoughts below:

Reminder: *You are safe to face yourself.*

Chapter 5
Finding My Voice

There is a difference between having a voice and using it.

For years, mine lived in my chest like a whisper afraid of its own echo. It was there when I was a little girl, child number five of nine, yet somehow always feeling like the only one standing alone. We didn't grow up under one roof. We didn't grow up in one safe place. Pieces of us were scattered at birth, and so was I. And when your life begins fragmented, it takes time to believe your voice even matters.

But this chapter isn't about fragmentation.

It's about reclamation.

I found my voice the day I decided I would no longer be walked over just because I had been wounded.

I found it in classrooms where statistics said I would fail.
I found it walking across that graduation stage, beating odds that were quietly whispered about me.

"She won't make it."
"She won't be anything."

But I did.

Graduating high school wasn't just about a diploma. It was proof that I was more than the environment that tried to define me. It was proof that I was not what happened to me. Every late night, every tear, every moment I doubted myself but kept going anyway, that was my voice learning to stand.

I learned to stand up for myself, even when standing came with consequences.

No matter how many times my aunt slapped me.
No matter how many times I was silenced with intimidation.
No matter how many times I was accused of things I didn't do.

There is something heavy about being hit not just with hands, but with lies.

When my aunt accused me of trying to sleep with her husband, the betrayal cut deeper than the accusation. Because the truth was uglier than the lie. He was the predator. I was the child. And she chose him.

She chose her husband over her niece.

That kind of rejection plants seeds of confusion in a young girl's heart. It makes you question your worth. It makes you wonder if protecting yourself will ever matter. It makes you feel disposable.

But what she didn't know was that every slap, every lie, every dismissal was chiseling something inside of me. It was shaping a strength she couldn't see.

And then there was my mother.

A woman battling drugs. A woman who would look me in my face and tell me I would never be anything. Words spoken through addiction. Words that didn't belong to the mother I longed for, but words that still pierced just the same.

Sometimes she would turn around and say she loved me.

And that contradiction is a special kind of pain.

Because as a daughter, I knew the drugs were speaking.
But as a child, I still needed my mother.

Knowing addiction was the enemy did not erase the ache. Understanding didn't cancel the longing. I belonged for my mother's love in ways I didn't even have language for at the time. I wanted her sober hugs. I wanted her proud smile. I wanted to hear, "You're going to be great," and believe it.

Instead, I had to become the voice I needed.

I had to learn to speak life over myself when no one else would.

Finding my voice wasn't loud at first. It didn't start with speeches or confrontations. It started with small rebellions against silence.

It started the day I said, "No."

No, you cannot treat me like that.
No, you cannot disrespect me.
No, you cannot define me by your brokenness.

It started the day I told someone, "That hurt me."

There is power in telling the truth about your pain without apologizing for it.

I used my voice by refusing to become bitter. That might be one of the hardest things I've ever done. Because bitterness is easy. Bitterness is protective. Bitterness says, "No one can hurt me again if I don't care."

But I cared.

I chose to show my heart anyway.

I chose softness without surrendering strength.
I chose accountability, not just for others, but for myself.

Finding my voice meant holding people accountable for how they treated me. But it also meant holding myself accountable for what I tolerated. It meant looking in the mirror and asking, "Why did I allow that?" Not to shame myself, but to free myself.

And then came the day that changed everything.

The day I told my grandmother the truth.

The words trembled in my throat. My body remembered what my mouth was trying to say. I told her I had been molested. I told her what had really been happening. I told her the lies that had been told about me.

That moment was terrifying.

Because when you have been silenced for so long, speaking feels like stepping off a cliff without knowing if there's ground beneath you.

But when the truth left my mouth, something shifted.

The shame that never belonged to me began to loosen its grip. The secrets that were suffocating me began to lose power. And for the first time, I felt what it meant to advocate for the little girl inside of me.

That was the day I decided I would never abandon myself again.

That was the day my voice stopped asking for permission.

I realized something powerful:
My silence had protected other people.
But my voice would protect me.

And from that point on, I chose to use it.

I use my voice now when I set boundaries.

I use it when I say, "This is unacceptable."
I use it when I say, "You hurt me."
I use it when I choose peace instead of revenge.

I use it when I walk away instead of staying where I am not valued.

My voice is not angry.
It is anchored.

It is not reckless.
It is rooted.

It carries the strength of a girl who survived what should have broken her.

To anyone reading this who has been silenced,

To anyone who was blamed for their own abuse,

To anyone who longed for love from someone who couldn't give it,

Your voice is not gone.

It is waiting.

You are allowed to speak.
You are allowed to tell the truth.
You are allowed to protect yourself.
You are allowed to say no.

You are allowed to heal without becoming hard.

Finding my voice didn't erase my past.

It redeemed it.

Because now, every time I speak, I speak for the girl who couldn't. Every time I stand, I stand for the child who was pushed down. Every time I choose love over bitterness, I defy everything that tried to make me small.

And this is only the beginning.

Because when you find your voice after being buried in silence, you don't just speak.

You rise.

And the next chapter?

It won't just be about surviving.

It will be about rising from the ruins.

PAUSE & REFLECT:

Where in your life have you been silent when you should have spoken up?

Write your thoughts below:

Reminder: *You no longer have to shrink yourself to be accepted.*

Chapter 6

Rising from the Ruins

Ruins don't happen overnight.

They happen slowly. Brick by brick. Trust by trust. Blow by blow. Word by word.

By the time I realized I was standing in the middle of wreckage, it wasn't just my childhood that felt shattered, it was the version of me that had survived by shrinking.

Finding my voice was the spark.

But rising from the ruins?

That was the fire.

Because once you speak the truth, you can't go back to pretending everything is whole.

You have to rebuild.

There is something no one tells you about survival.

Survival keeps you alive.

But it does not automatically make you free.

For years, I survived.

I survived the slaps.

I survived the lies.

I survived being accused instead of protected.

I survived longing for a sober mother.

I survived abuse that should have never touched a child.

But surviving meant I was still carrying rubble inside me.

And rubble is heavy.

It shows up in how you love.

It shows up in what you tolerate.

It shows up in how quickly you blame yourself.

It shows up in the way you brace for impact even when no one is swinging.

Rising required something different.

It required excavation.

I had to dig through the lies that were planted in me.

“You’re nothing.”

“You’re fast.”

“You’re trouble.”

“You’re dramatic.”

“You’re too much.”

Those words weren’t just spoken over me. They were layered into my foundation.

So, I had to tear them out.

And tearing out lies feels violent at first. Because when you’ve heard something long enough, it starts to sound like truth.

But I began replacing them.

I am worthy.

I am not responsible for grown men's sin.

I am not what was done to me.

I am not the addiction that raised me.

I am not the silence that protected others.

I am rebuilding.

Rising from the ruins meant grieving what I never had.

That part is important.

You cannot rise if you refuse to mourn.

I had to mourn the mother I deserved.

The aunt who should have defended me.

The safe childhood that was stolen.

The version of myself that learned to smile through pain.

Grief is not weakness.

Grief is the ceremony of letting go.

And once I allowed myself to grieve, something beautiful happened:

I stopped trying to earn love from people who were incapable of giving it.

That was revolutionary.

Because so much of my life had been spent performing for acceptance. Being strong. Being helpful. Being forgiving. Being quiet. Being "the bigger person."

Rising meant I no longer needed to audition for love.

If you cannot see my value, that is not my assignment to fix.

There is power in rebuilding yourself intentionally.

I began choosing environments that felt safe.

I began setting boundaries without overexplaining.

I began noticing red flags instead of romanticizing them.

I began trusting my instincts instead of doubting them.

The same girl who once felt voiceless became a woman who speaks with clarity.

The same girl who once felt disposable became a woman who knows she is chosen.

The same girl who once questioned her worth now understands she survived things that could have buried her, and she is still standing.

That is not weakness.

That is architecture.

Ruins are evidence that something collapsed.

But they are also evidence that something once stood.

And if it stood once, it can stand again, stronger.

I am not rebuilding the same girl.

I am rebuilding with wisdom.

With discernment.

With boundaries.

With faith.

With accountability.

Yes, accountability.

Because rising from the ruins also meant facing the ways I coped.

It meant admitting when I allowed people to overstep.

It meant recognizing when I stayed too long.

It meant forgiving myself for not knowing better when I was younger.

You cannot punish yourself into healing.

You heal by choosing differently.

And I am choosing differently.

There is something powerful about a woman who has seen the worst and still chooses softness.

I did not let bitterness win.

That alone is a miracle.

It would have been easy to harden.

To become cold.

To distrust everyone.

To treat the world the way it treated me.

But I refused.

Because rising is not about revenge.

It is about restoration.

It is about looking at the wreckage and saying:

“You didn’t destroy me. You revealed me.”

Every scar tells a story of survival.

Every boundary tells a story of growth.

Every “no” tells a story of self-respect.

Every tear I allowed myself to cry tells a story of courage.

I am not ashamed of my ruins.

They built my resilience.

To the one reading this who feels buried under what happened to you,

You are not the rubble.

You are the rebuilder.

You are allowed to start over.

You are allowed to outgrow people.

You are allowed to heal loudly.

You are allowed to take up space.

You are allowed to rise even if no one apologizes.

Closure is not always a conversation.

Sometimes closure is elevation.

Sometimes closure is peace.

Sometimes closure is walking forward without looking back.

Rising from the ruins is not glamorous.

It is messy.

It is layered.

It is painful.

It is sacred.

It looks like therapy.

It looks like prayer.

It looks like cutting ties.

It looks like forgiving without reconciling.

It looks like choosing yourself over chaos.

And when you rise, people who benefited from your brokenness may not recognize you.

That's okay.

You are not rebuilding for their comfort.

You are rebuilding for your freedom.

I am no longer the girl waiting to be saved.

I am the woman who saved herself by telling the truth.

The woman who protected her inner child.

The woman who chose healing over hiding.

The woman who turned ruins into foundation.

And this is what I know now:

What tried to bury me actually planted me.

And planted things?

They rise.

PAUSE & REFLECT:

What did you survive that should have broken you, but didn't?

Write your thoughts below:

Reminder: *You are still here for a reason.*

Chapter 7
Treasure in the Jars of Clay

There is a certain fragility in being human that most people hide.
We walk through the world as though our cracks are shameful secrets, as if the places where we break define us instead of the light that escapes through them.

I have always been a jar of clay.

Rough edges. Cracks no one wanted to notice. Hollow spaces I tried to fill with approval, with love, with the idea that if I could just be enough, maybe the world would stop hurting me.

But clay breaks.

It doesn't matter how carefully it's molded, how polished it's made to look, life has a way of testing you until cracks appear. My cracks came early.

I wasn't graphic in telling my story. I didn't need to be. Some experiences are too raw for words. Some scars are etched into your soul so deeply that no sentence could ever hold them. But that doesn't mean they aren't there. That doesn't mean they didn't shape me. That doesn't mean they didn't leave room for treasure.

Because treasure doesn't come in spite of the clay, it comes through it.

I am proof of that.

Every time I wanted to disappear, to shrink, to pretend the abuse, the lies, the neglect never happened, I discovered that the emptiness inside me wasn't a void to fear; it was a vessel. And vessels are meant to be filled.

Filled with love, yes.
Filled with forgiveness, yes.
Filled with truth, yes.

But first, filled with self-recognition.

I had to look into my own soul and admit what I had endured. I had to whisper the truth to the girl who had been silenced for so long:

"You survived this. You are still here. You are more than what happened to you."

And that was the first treasure.

The treasure of acknowledging that my value didn't depend on the hands that hurt me or the people who abandoned me. My value was not in their choices. My value was in the one constant I carried inside: myself.

Every scar, every shame, every disappointment became gold.

I began to see it, not in an instant, but slowly, like sunlight filtering through cracks in a weathered jar.

There is something holy about brokenness when it is embraced instead of hidden.

Because when you embrace your cracks, you discover that they are not weaknesses, they are the channels for light to enter.

I began to collect the treasures hidden in my jars of clay:

- ❖ The resilience that kept me standing when everyone expected me to fall.
- ❖ The courage to speak my truth even when my voice trembled.
- ❖ The compassion that bloomed from witnessing pain I could have let harden me.
- ❖ The wisdom that only comes from surviving what no one should have to survive.
- ❖ The self-love I fought for every day, against voices that told me I was unworthy.

And here is the paradox that shook me to my core: the more broken I felt, the more treasure I found.

I began to realize that people relate to this because everyone is a jar of clay in some form.

Every person you see smiling, walking confidently, holding their head high, they too have cracks. Their treasure is hidden in the places they've been shattered. The mother working two jobs just to make ends meet, her hands are calloused, but inside, she carries grace. The friend who stayed silent when they should have spoken, they carry wisdom born from regret. The person you envy, their victories are stacked atop unseen struggles.

We all carry treasure in our clay.

And the secret is this: we are only valuable because we are fragile.
We only shine because we are broken.
We only connect because our emptiness makes space for light, for love, for understanding to fill us and overflow to others.

I have learned that my jars of clay are not accidents. They are designs.

The cracks, the breaks, the moments I wanted to disappear, they are intentional places for light to enter, for treasure to be revealed, for truth to live.

So, I carry my jars proudly now.
I show the world my cracks without shame.
I embrace the weight of what I have endured because inside, there is treasure.

And here is the final revelation:

The world may try to measure you by perfection, by how polished your exterior looks.
But the Creator doesn't.
He measures you by the treasure within.

Every scar I own, every tear I've cried, every injustice I've endured, they are the proof of treasure.
Treasure that cannot be stolen. Treasure that cannot be replicated. Treasure that cannot be erased.

And when someone reads this, I want them to clutch their pearls, not out of horror, but out of awe.

Awe that even in the brokenness, there is purpose.
Awe that even in the silence, there is voice.
Awe that even in the ruins, there is treasure.

My jars of clay are many. My jars of clay are cracked.
But they are filled, overflowing with light, hope, and everything that makes me unshakable.

And I have learned the most important truth:

You are treasure. Your cracks are treasure. Your life, every jagged, painful, glorious part of it, is treasure.

PAUSE & REFLECT:

What strength or purpose has come from what you've been through?

Write your thoughts below:

Reminder: *There is purpose in what you've been through.*

Chapter 8

Unshakable Faith

Building a Life That Cannot Be Moved

Faith is not born in comfort.

Faith is forged in the storm.

By this point in my journey, I was no stranger to pain. Life had introduced me to its harshest realities, betrayal that cut deeper than words, abandonment that left echoes in empty spaces, and voices that tried to convince me I wasn't enough. I had walked through fire more times than I could count, sometimes by choice, but often because life gave me no other option.

And still… I'm here.

Not untouched. Not unscarred.

But unshakable.

Because somewhere in the middle of the chaos, I discovered a truth that changed everything: unshakable faith doesn't mean the storm won't come, it means you develop roots deep enough that no storm can uproot you.

I often think about what it means to be like jars of clay, fragile, imperfect, and easily broken, yet chosen to carry something so divine. There's something humbling about knowing that God didn't wait for me to be flawless before using me. He didn't discard me because of my cracks. Instead, He chose me *because* of them.

Those cracks? They became openings.

Openings for His light to shine through.

Openings for grace to rest on me.

Openings for His strength to show up where mine ran out.

I am fragile clay, yes, but I carry something far greater than my fragility. I carry purpose. I carry power. I carry God.

And that changes everything.

When life shakes me, I don't fall apart the way I used to. Not because I'm strong on my own, but because I've learned where my strength comes from.

God is not just present when life is good.

He is closest when life is hardest.

He is my refuge, not because He removes the storm, but because He anchors me in the middle of it.

Faith is a choice.

And not the easy kind.

It is waking up on days when your heart feels heavy and choosing to believe anyway.

It is standing tall when everything around you is trying to knock you down.

It is trusting God when the outcome doesn't make sense, when the timing feels off, and when the silence feels loud.

Faith is not passive, it is intentional.

It is choosing hope when despair feels more realistic.

It is choosing peace when chaos feels justified.

It is choosing God, even when life feels like it's choosing everything else over you.

Anyone can believe when life is good. That doesn't require faith, that requires comfort.

But real faith?

Real faith is built in the moments that break you.

The betrayals.

The disappointments.

The seasons where you feel unseen, unheard, and forgotten.

Those are the moments that define you.

Because if you can still choose God there, if you can still trust Him there, you begin to realize that your foundation is no longer fragile.

It is firm.

Building a life that cannot be moved requires intention.

It doesn't happen by accident. It doesn't come from wishing things were easier. It comes from doing the hard, internal work, the kind nobody sees but God.

I had to sit with myself and ask questions that were uncomfortable but necessary:

Am I holding on to pain that God is asking me to release?

Am I choosing peace, or am I feeding my wounds?

Am I shrinking myself to make others comfortable, or am I standing in my truth?

Am I setting boundaries that protect my spirit, even when it disappoints others?

Am I trusting God's timing… or rushing ahead because I'm afraid of waiting?

These weren't easy questions.

But they were necessary for growth.

Because faith isn't just about what you say you believe, it's about how you live when life tests what you believe.

I had to learn that faith doesn't mean perfection.

It doesn't mean I always get it right.

It doesn't mean life suddenly becomes fair.

It doesn't mean I don't feel pain, anger, or disappointment.

Faith means I don't let those things define me.

Faith means I don't allow my circumstances to dictate my identity.

Faith means I don't let temporary seasons convince me of permanent lies.

It means I stand, no matter what.

There is a difference between hearing truth and living it.

It's one thing to know God's Word.

It's another thing to build your life on it.

Because when the storms come, and they will come, only what is built on a solid foundation will remain.

I've seen what happens when life is built on unstable ground—on people, on validation, on temporary things. It collapses when pressure comes.

But when your life is built on faith, real, tested, stretched faith it doesn't, collapse.

It stands.

Not because the winds didn't blow.

Not because the rain didn't fall.

But because the foundation was strong enough to hold it all together.

Today, I don't fear the storm the way I used to.

Not because storms don't hurt.

But because I know they don't have the power to destroy me.

I've been through too much.

I've survived too much.

I've seen God move too many times.

And now I understand:

What was meant to break me… built me.

What was meant to shake me… strengthened me.

What was meant to destroy me… deepened my faith.

I am still standing.

Stronger.

Wiser.

Rooted.

Unshakable.

Because my life is no longer built on what I see.

It's built on what I believe.

And that… cannot be moved.

PAUSE & REFLECT:

What are you still holding on to that is keeping you from becoming who you're meant to be?

Write your thoughts below:

Reminder: *You cannot heal what you continue to hold on to.*

Conclusion

Whole, Not Perfect

If you've made it here, you've already done something powerful, you stayed.

Through every page, every memory, every truth that may have felt too heavy to carry… you stayed. And that alone says something about you. It says you are stronger than you realize.

Because this journey, my journey, was never just about me.

It was about you too.

This story began with cracks.

Not the kind you can easily fix or hide, but the kind that runs deep. The kind that shapes how you see yourself, how you love, how you trust, how you survive.

For a long time, I believed those cracks made me broken beyond repair. I thought I had to hide them, cover them up, pretend they didn't exist just to be accepted… just to feel worthy.

But what I've learned is this:

Those cracks were never the end of me.

They were the beginning.

Every chapter you've read is a piece of becoming.

From surviving what tried to take me out…

To fighting to be seen when I felt invisible…

To confronting the reflection of who I thought I was…

To finding my voice after years of silence…

To rising from places, I never thought I'd escape…

To realizing that even in my fragility, I still carried something valuable…

Every moment led me here.

Not perfect.

Not untouched.

But whole.

Wholeness is not what I thought it would be.

It's not having it all together.

It's not waking up every day without pain.

It's not being free from struggle or scars.

Wholeness is acceptance.

It's looking at every part of yourself, the healed parts, the healing parts, and even the parts that still hurt, and choosing not to reject any of it.

It's understanding that your story doesn't disqualify you.

It qualifies you.

There is power in your story.

Even the parts you wish you could erase.

Even the chapters you don't talk about.

Even the moments that made you question everything.

Because those moments didn't just happen *to* you.

They shaped you.

They refined you.

They revealed strength in you that comfort never could.

Healing is not a destination.

It is a decision you make, over and over again.

Some days it looks like progress.

Other days it looks like simply getting out of bed and choosing not to give up.

And both count.

Give yourself permission to heal at your pace.

Give yourself grace on the days it feels heavy.

Give yourself credit for how far you've come.

Because you have come far.

You are not what happened to you.

You are not the pain.

You are not the rejection.

You are not the mistakes.

You are not the voices that tried to define you.

You are what you chose to become in spite of it.

And that is powerful.

If there is anything I want you to take from this book, it's this:

You don't have to be perfect to be whole.

You don't have to have all the answers to move forward.

You don't have to erase your past to step into your future.

You just have to keep going.

Keep healing.

Keep choosing yourself.

Keep choosing God.

Keep believing that your life still has purpose, no matter what it has looked like up until now.

I am no longer trying to fix myself into something I was never meant to be.

I am no longer hiding the parts of me that tell my truth.

I am no longer waiting for perfection to feel worthy.

I am whole.

And you can be too.

This is not the end.

This is the part where you take everything you've read… everything you've felt… and begin to write your own next chapter.

One rooted in truth.

One grounded in faith.

One shaped by healing.

Because your story is still being written.

And it deserves a beautiful ending.

FINAL REFLECTION

Who are you becoming from this moment forward?

Write your thoughts below:

Reminder: *You are not who you were, you are who you choose to become.*

A Letter to You

If you've made it this far…

I want you to pause for a moment.

Not to rush to the next thing.

Not to skim past this page.

But to really sit here with yourself.

Because finishing this book wasn't just about turning pages…

It was about facing parts of yourself that you may not always have the courage to confront.

And for that, I honor you.

I don't know your full story.

I don't know every tear you've cried in private…

Every moment you had to be strong when you felt like falling apart…

Every time you smiled on the outside while silently breaking within…

But I do know this:

You didn't pick this book by accident.

Something in you is searching.

Something in you is healing.

Something in you is ready.

There are parts of life that change us.

The kind of experiences that don't just pass through… they stay.

They reshape how we see ourselves, how we love, how we trust, how we show up in the world.

And if you're not careful, they can convince you of things that were never true:

That you are too broken.

That you are too much.

That you are not enough.

That what you've been through defines who you are.

But I need you to hear me clearly:

That is not your truth.

You are not the pain you've experienced.

You are not the abandonment.

You are not the rejection.

You are not the mistakes.

You are not the labels that were placed on you.

You are the one who survived it.

You are the one who kept going.

You are the one who is still here.

And that alone means there is purpose attached to your life.

Healing is not easy.

It will require you to revisit places you tried to forget.

It will require you to release things you've held onto for years.

It will require you to be honest with yourself in ways that feel uncomfortable.

But healing is also where you meet yourself again.

Not the version shaped by survival…

But the version rooted in truth.

You don't have to rush your healing.

You don't have to have it all figured out.

You don't have to wake up tomorrow and be completely whole.

Take it one step at a time.

One decision at a time.

One moment of honesty at a time.

One act of choosing yourself at a time.

That is enough.

There will be days where it feels heavy again.

Days where old thoughts try to return.

Days where doubt feels louder than faith.

Days where you question your progress.

On those days, remember this:

Growth is not always loud.

Healing is not always visible.

But that doesn't mean it isn't happening.

I want you to give yourself something today.

Grace.

Grace for what you didn't know then.

Grace for the choices you made while trying to survive.

Grace for the parts of you that are still healing.

You deserve that.

And as you move forward from this book, I want you to carry this with you:

You are allowed to become.

You are allowed to outgrow people, places, and patterns that no longer align with who you are becoming.

You are allowed to set boundaries without guilt.

You are allowed to choose peace—even if it disappoints others.

You are allowed to rebuild your life on your terms.

Most importantly…

You are allowed to heal.

Fully.

Completely.

Unapologetically.

My prayer for you is not that life becomes perfect.

But that you become rooted.

Rooted in truth.

Rooted in faith.

Rooted in a deep understanding that no matter what you've been through—you are still worthy, still chosen, and still becoming everything you were created to be.

This is not the end of your story.

This is the part where you take everything you've faced…
everything you've learned… everything you've survived…

And you build something new from it.

Something stronger.

Something healthier.

Something aligned.

Something whole.

And if no one has told you this…

I'm proud of you.

For staying.

For trying.

For not giving up even when it felt easier to.

Keep going.

— Carmila T.

A Prayer for Healing, Releasing, and Becoming

Heavenly Father,

We come before You not perfect, not polished, not pretending

but as we are.

With open hearts…

with hidden wounds…

With questions we don't always have the words to ask.

God, you see every reader of these pages.

You know their story, the parts they share and the parts they hide.

You know the weight they've been carrying, the silent battles they've been fighting, and the moments they almost gave up.

And yet… they are still here.

So, Father, I ask right now that You meet them in this very moment.

Not later.

Not someday.

But right here, right now.

God, begin to break every chain that has held them captive.

Every lie that told them they weren't enough

break it.

Every voice that tried to define them by their past

silence it.

Every burden they were never meant to carry

lift it.

Lord, remove the weight of guilt, shame, rejection, and fear.

Strip away everything that is not like You.

Father, I declare healing over their mind.

Where there has been confusion bring clarity.

Where there has been anxiety bring peace.

Where there has been overthinking—bring stillness.

Heal their thoughts.

Renew their mind.

Restore their identity.

Let them begin to see themselves the way You see them

chosen, worthy, whole.

God, I speak healing over their heart.

Every place that was broken by people…

every scar left by words…

every wound caused by abandonment…

Father, touch those places.

Not just on the surface

but deep within.

Remove the pain they've normalized.

Heal the hurt they've learned to live with.

And replace it with Your love.

Lord, give them the strength to release what they've been holding on to.

The pain.

The resentment.

The past.

The version of themselves they've outgrown.

Give them the courage to let it go—fully and completely.

Because what You have for them requires room.

And they cannot carry both the past and their purpose at the same time.

Father, awaken something new within them.

A new mindset.

A new level of faith.

A new level of confidence.

Let this moment mark a turning point in their life.

Where they no longer settle for less than what You've called them to be.

Where they no longer shrink themselves to fit spaces they've outgrown.

Where they begin to walk boldly in who they are becoming.

God, I declare that they are not stuck.

They are not behind.

They are not forgotten.

They are being prepared.

Everything they've been through is being used—

for growth, for purpose, for transformation.

Lord, plant them in You.

Make them unshakable.

Even when life feels uncertain.

Even when the storm comes.

Let their faith be rooted so deeply in You

that nothing can move them.

And Father, from this moment forward—

Let them walk differently.

Let them think differently.

Let them see themselves differently.

Let them rise with strength.

Let them move with purpose.

Let them live with intention.

We surrender every burden.

We release every weight.

We trust you with every piece of our story.

And we receive

Your peace,

Your healing,

Your restoration,

Your power.

In Jesus' name,

Amen.

DECLARATION

I AM BECOMING

I am not my past.

I am not my pain.

I am not the things I've been through.

I am becoming.

I am becoming whole—even as I heal.

I am becoming stronger—even when it feels hard.

I am becoming more aligned with who I was created to be.

I release what no longer serves me.

I let go of what tried to break me.

I walk away from what no longer aligns with my growth.

I choose peace over chaos.

I choose healing over hiding.

I choose growth over staying the same.

I am worthy.

I am enough.

I am chosen.

I will no longer shrink myself to fit places I've outgrown.

I will no longer silence myself to make others comfortable.

I will no longer carry what God has asked me to release.

I trust the process of my healing.

I trust the timing of my life.

I trust that everything I've been through is working for me not against me.

My past does not define me.

My pain did not destroy me.

My story is still being written.

I am rising.

I am healing.

I am becoming.

From this moment forward

I will walk in purpose.

I will move with intention.

I will live as the person I am becoming.

Read this out loud daily. Let it take root within you.

DAILY AFFIRMATIONS

I am worthy of love, peace, and happiness

I am not defined by my past

I am enough exactly as I am

I am healing, even when it doesn't feel like it

I release what no longer serves me

I give myself permission to move forward

I choose growth over comfort

I trust the process of my life

I have the power to rewrite my story

My voice matters

I no longer shrink myself for others

I stand firm in who I am

God is working in my life, even when I don't see it

I trust God's timing over my own

I am walking by faith, not by fear

I am becoming who I was created to be

My life has purpose and meaning

I am rising beyond everything that tried to break me

Speak these over your life daily until you begin to believe them.

SCRIPTURES FOR HEALINGAND BECOMING

Jeremiah 29:11

"For I know the plans I have for you," declares the Lord...

Psalm 147:3

"He heals the brokenhearted and binds up their wounds."

Isaiah 41:10

"Do not fear, for I am with you..."

Romans 12:2

"Be transformed by the renewing of your mind."

Isaiah 43:18-19

"Forget the former things... I am doing a new thing."

Proverbs 3:5-6

"Trust in the Lord with all your heart..."

Romans 8:28

"All things work together for good..."

2 Corinthians 5:17

"If anyone is in Christ, he is a new creation"

SCRIPTURES FOR STRENGTH, AUTHORITY, AND TRANSFORMATION

Isaiah 54:17

"No weapon formed against you shall prosper..."

2 Timothy 1:7

"For God has not given us a spirit of fear, but of power, love, and a sound mind."

Joel 2:25

"I will restore to you the years that the locust has eaten..."

Ephesians 3:20

"Now unto Him who is able to do exceedingly abundantly above all that we ask or think..."

Philippians 1:6

"He who began a good work in you will carry it on to completion..."

Psalm 23:4

"Even though I walk through the valley... I will fear no evil, for You are with me."

Micah 7:8

"Though I have fallen, I will rise..."

Deuteronomy 28:13

"The Lord will make you the head and not the tail..."

Declare these over your life. Walk in them boldly. This is your season of becoming.

ABOUT THE AUTHOR

Carmila is a child of God first.

Before anything she does, before any title she carries that is who she is.

She is a mother, a loving sister, a daughter, and a friend. She is an entrepreneur, a realtor, and a nail technician. But beyond all of that, she is a woman who has walked through life, felt its weight, and made the decision to heal.

Her journey has not been easy.

She has faced moments that tried to break her, seasons that tested her strength, and experiences that could have shaped her into someone unrecognizable. But instead of allowing her pain to define her, she chose to confront it… to grow through it… and to rise from it.

She did the work.

The quiet, uncomfortable, unseen work of healing.

And somewhere along that journey she found peace.

Not a perfect life.

Not a life without challenges.

But a peace that grounds her, strengthens her, and reminds her of who she is, even on the hard days.

This book was written from that place.

A place of truth.

A place of reflection.

A place of becoming.

Carmila doesn't claim to have all the answers. She is still growing, still learning, still healing in her own ways. But what she does know is this:

Healing is possible.

Peace is possible.

And you are not too far gone to become who you were created to be.

Her heart is to remind others that they are not broken, they are becoming.

STAY CONNECTED

If you've made it to this page…

I want you to know something from my heart:

I'm not leaving you here.

This journey doesn't end when this book ends.

Healing doesn't stop on the last page.

And growth doesn't happen all at once.

I'm walking with you.

Through the healing.

Through the hard days.

Through the becoming.

If you saw yourself in these pages, if something in you shifted, if you've made the decision to grow and heal—please know you are not alone in this.

This is only the beginning.

There is more.

More healing.

More growth.

More truth.

More of you to discover.

And yes… there's another book coming.

One that will go even deeper.

One that will continue this journey with you.

So, stay connected. Stay close.

Let's keep growing together. I'm still with you, even after the book closes.

Notes:

I stopped trying to fix what broke me and allowed it to build me.

www.ingramcontent.com/pod-product-compliance
Lightning Source LLC
LaVergne TN
LVHW090523110826
845146LV00003B/964
9798995694007